Pablo's Junior Rangers

THE RAINFOREST ADVENTURE

Olivia Stanfield

Kit Turner

KID'S BLUFF BOOKS

No parts of this book may be reproduced without the written permission of the publisher.
For more information, contact the publisher at info@kidsbluffbooks.com
Kid's Bluff Books and the colophon are registered trademarks of Kid's Bluff Books.

ISBN 978-1-965063-08-8.
LCCN 2025901780

The characters and events portrayed in this book are fictitious. Any similarity to real persons, living or dead, is purely coincidental and not intended by the author.

Published by Kid's Bluff Books
8401 Mayland Drive, Suite 4241
Richmond, VA 23294
www.kidsbluffbooks.com

Hola! Welcome to **Argentina and Iguazú National Park,**
a steamy subtropical rainforest.
I'm Pablo the park ranger and your host.
As a ranger, my job is to track, observe and protect the wildlife
that make the park their home.

Today, my mission is to view
the jaguars that live
in the rainforest.
I'll check on our
other fauna, too.

Fauna is another
word for wildlife.

Would you like to be a Junior Ranger?
Great. We'll have to **stay very quiet**
and keep our **eyes wide open.**
I should warn you, my eyesight is terrible.
Will you let me know if you spot a jaguar?
Thanks, I'd appreciate it.

Would you like to see where exactly we are on the globe?
Right here, where the north-east of Argentina meets the south of Paraguay and Brazil.

Did you lose me? Sorry about that, Junior Ranger,
I've been practicing blending in with my surroundings.
That's how park rangers observe fauna without disturbing them.
Do you know what hiding in plain sight is called?

That's right, camouflage. I'm impressed.
Unfortunately, jaguars and their spotted coats
 are extremely good at using camouflage,
so we've got our work cut out for us.
Jaguars are an endangered species;
that means there are not many left in the wild.
They are also very good at hiding in plain sight,
so I could use your help.

Do you like the view?
This is Iguazú Falls
(pronounced ee-gwuh-zoo in English),
the largest group of waterfalls in the world.

National Parks, like Iguazú, are great places to visit.
Here, wildlife and their homes, called habitats, are protected.
That means no hunting or trapping.
Rangers, like myself, learn about the park's fauna through observation.
We also work hard to keep them safe.

It's just after dawn, our noisiest residents are in the trees nearby.
Let's get started!

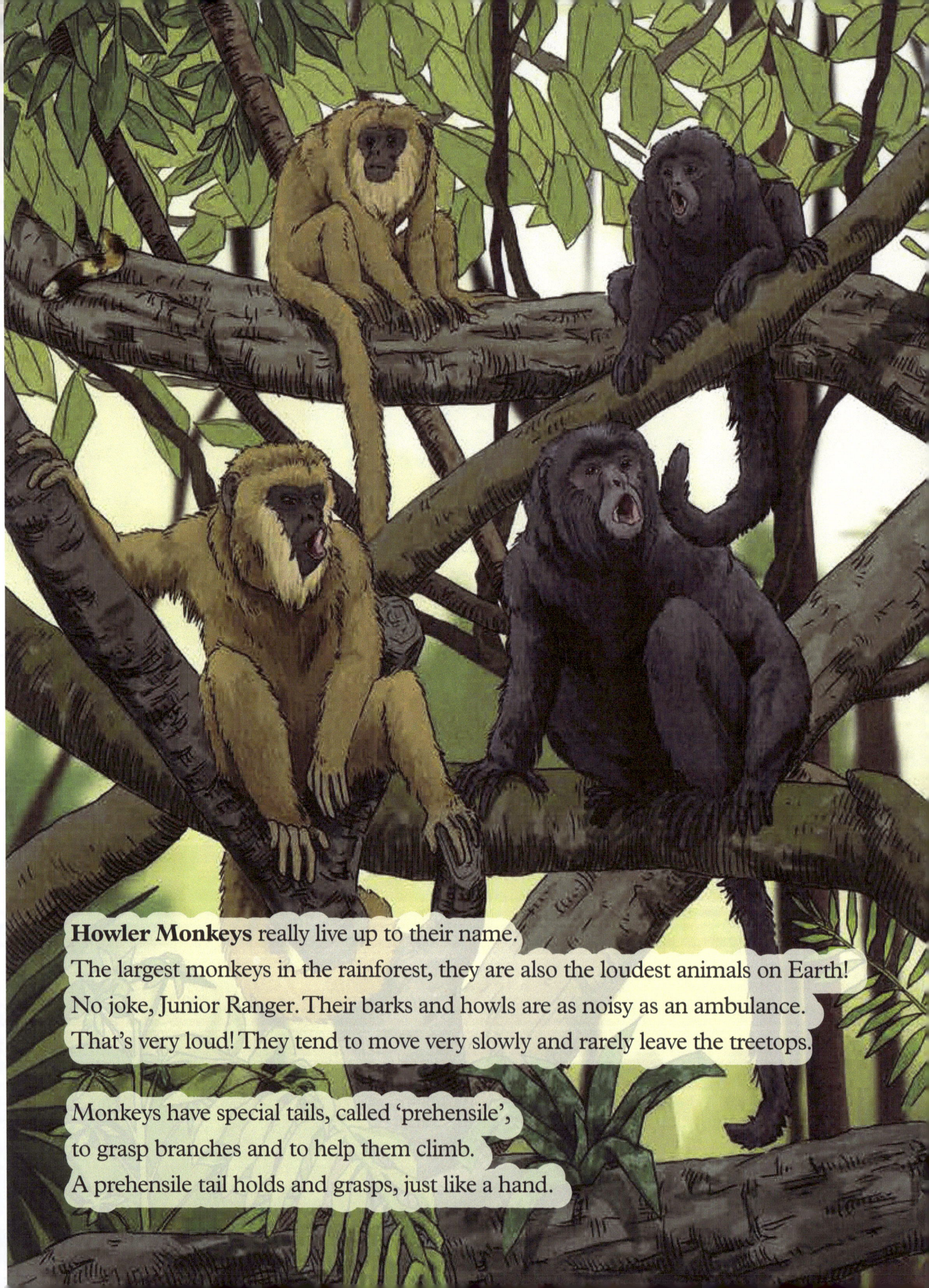

Howler Monkeys really live up to their name.
The largest monkeys in the rainforest, they are also the loudest animals on Earth!
No joke, Junior Ranger. Their barks and howls are as noisy as an ambulance.
That's very loud! They tend to move very slowly and rarely leave the treetops.

Monkeys have special tails, called 'prehensile',
to grasp branches and to help them climb.
A prehensile tail holds and grasps, just like a hand.

Do you see the baby? All howlers are born with golden-brown fur. As they grow, the male's fur darkens and turns black. Females stay golden or turn a reddish brown. Can you tell which ones are which?

Capuchin Monkeys are always on the go, unlike their howler cousins. Small and fast, they have tons of energy! While they are different in many ways, both species have prehensile tails to help them climb and swing. Like howlers, capuchins live high above the ground, rarely leaving the treetops.

Capuchins are not as loud as howlers, which is a relief! But they are very chatty. Their high-pitched calls sound like a small bird's song.

Newborn capuchins feel safest riding on their mother's chest.
Can you find the infant riding on its mother´s back?
It is about three months old.
The youngsters we see here are almost a year old.
They´ve learned to climb on their own.

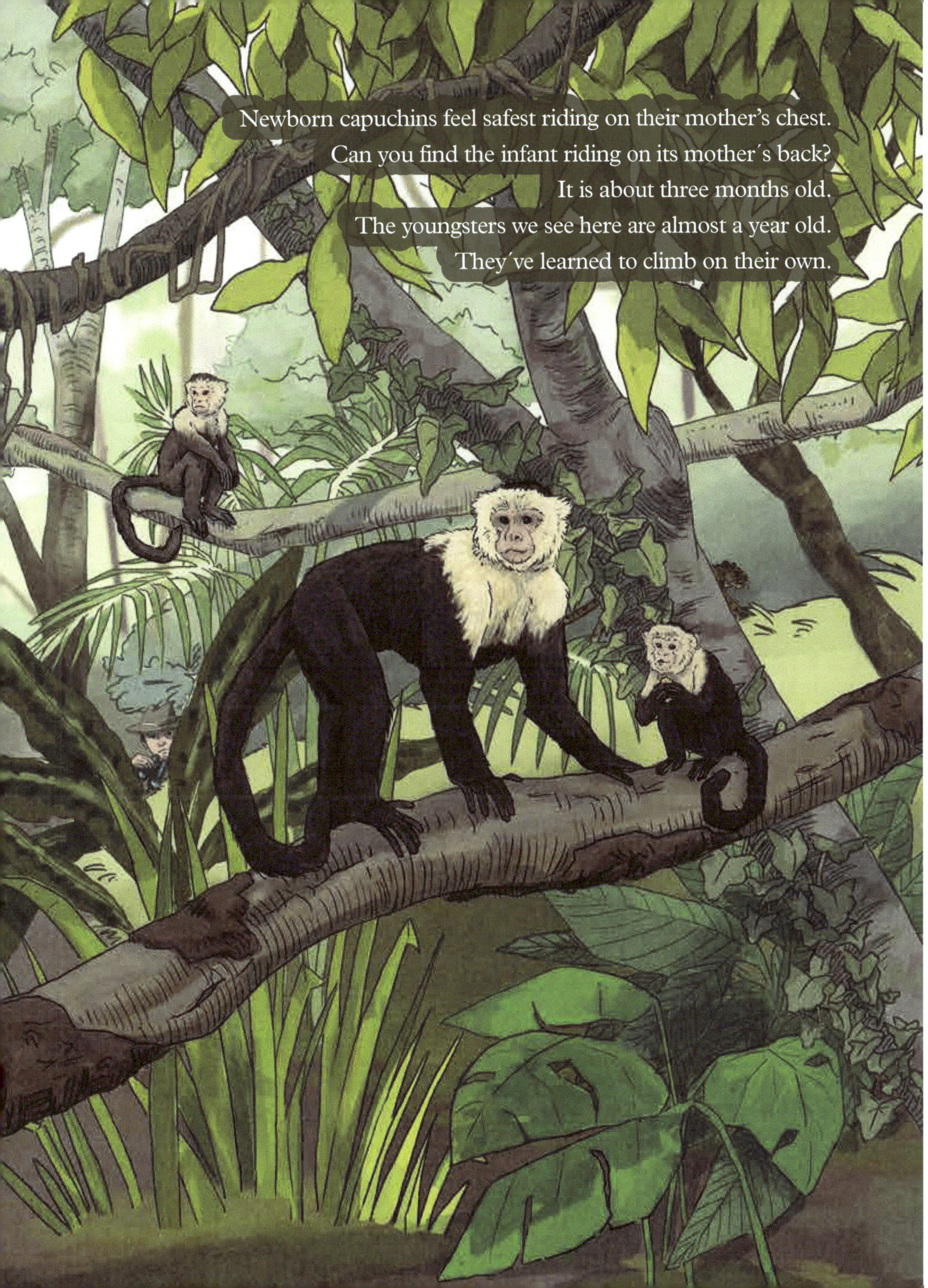

Have you ever seen one of these, Junior Ranger?
These are **Giant Anteaters**, the largest of their kind
and one of our most unique residents.

That long head is mostly a big snout, that's an animal's nose and mouth.
Anteaters don't have great eyesight, just like me.
But their super snout provides them with an amazing sense of smell.
That's how they track down their favorite snack.

Can you guess what that is, Junior Ranger?

Yes, ants! Anteaters love to eat ants.
Their super-strong sense of smell helps them locate an anthill.
Then, they rip the hill open with their strong claws.
That's when the fun begins.
They dip their extra-long tongue into the tunnels to pull out the bugs.
Doesn't that sound delicious?

Anteater babies are called pups. Just like monkey infants, this pup rides on its mother's back for safety.
The anteater mother lines up the pup's stripes with her own, making it hard to spot. What is that an example of, Junior Ranger?

You got it, camouflage. Well done!

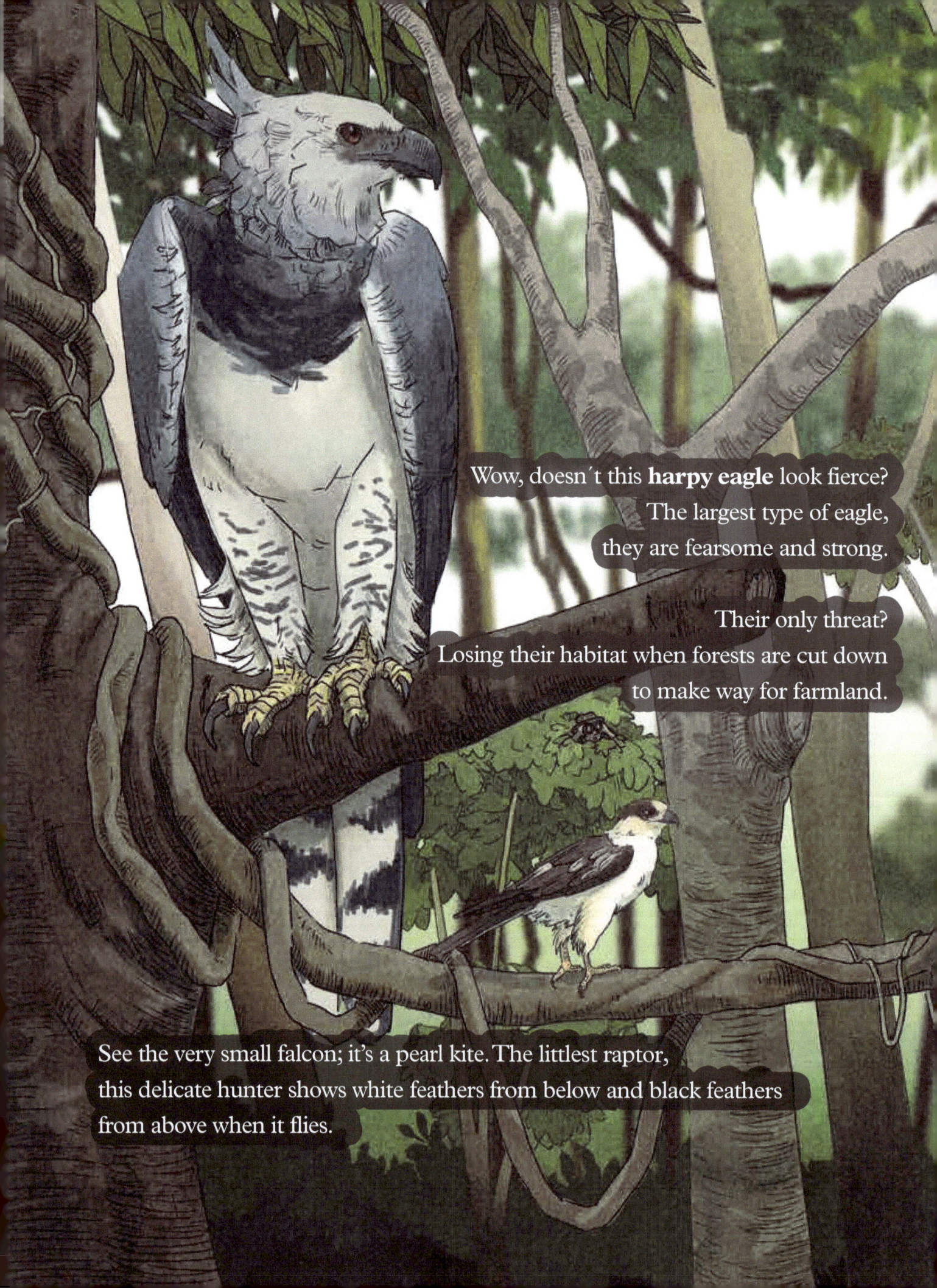

Wow, doesn't this **harpy eagle** look fierce?
The largest type of eagle,
they are fearsome and strong.

Their only threat?
Losing their habitat when forests are cut down
to make way for farmland.

See the very small falcon; it's a pearl kite. The littlest raptor,
this delicate hunter shows white feathers from below and black feathers
from above when it flies.

Did you know the large beak of the **toucan** is hollow and lightweight?
Unlike many birds, male and female toucans are identical.
So it's hard to tell which is which.

The **green and red macaw**
is a true symbolof the rainforest.
These beauties are not endangered,
though it is illegal to have them
as pets here in Argentina.
Which animal that we hope
to spot today is endangered?

That's right, the jaguar! You've been so quiet
that I can hear a stream nearby. Jaguars love water, did you know that?
Most species of felines or cats don't, but jaguars spend a lot of time in and
around rivers and streams. Maybe we'll get lucky?

Giant river otters, I should have guessed.
They are almost as big as us, they grow up to six feet long.
The largest members of the Weasel family,
otters use their strong tails to swim and dive.
Great fishers, they eat crabs, fish and small reptiles.

Junior Ranger, can you find the otter pups?
Also called cubs, they are born in dry dens on land.
Otter mothers are always on the look-out for jaguars
on the riverbanks trying to catch a careless pup,
so I don't think we'll find one here.
Let's try downstream, follow me.

Look, Caimans! We´ve found two different types.
Both love to bask in the sun and it's noon, their favorite time of day.

Closely related to alligators,
caimans are smaller and faster with sharper teeth.
They have overlapping scales that move like a suit of armor.

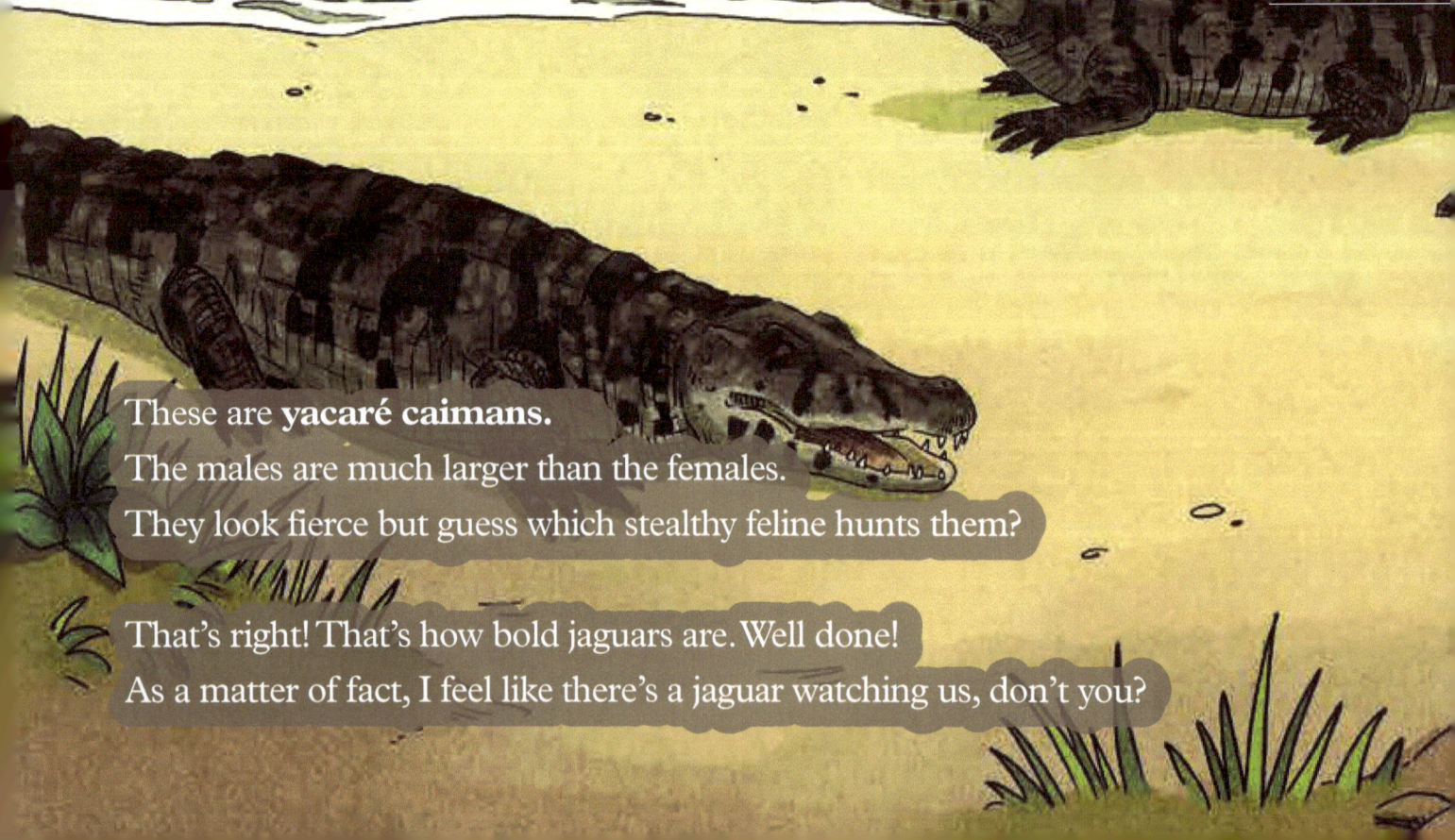

These are **yacaré caimans.**
The males are much larger than the females.
They look fierce but guess which stealthy feline hunts them?

That's right! That's how bold jaguars are. Well done!
As a matter of fact, I feel like there's a jaguar watching us, don't you?

The **broad-nosed caiman** carries her young in her mouth.
After hatching her eggs in a large nest, she'll try to care for them.
That includes a special ride to keep them safe.
Young caiman are prey to many species,
only a few survive to adulthood.

Let's go, Junior Ranger,
I think we'll have better luck in the shade.

I should have known we'd find these guys cooling off.
Capybaras are the largest living rodents.
Like their cousin, the guinea pig, they are native to South America.
These furry friends grow up to four feet long and they love the water.

Unlike most wildlife, capybaras have adapted to sharing habitats with humans.
They roam free in zoos and public parks in cities in Latin America.
They can also be found in the neighborhoods built
on marshes where they lived before humans arrived.

Capybaras are social, unlike the jaguar we are looking for.
See the pups? They are fed and nursed by all the females in the herd, not
just their birth-mothers.
That means everyone takes care of everyone. Isn't that a cool rule?

Iguazú has hundreds of species of butterflies.
This is a blue morpho, one of the largest.
It comes in many glimmering shades of electric blue.

Watch out for the snake, Junior Ranger, that's a **yarará**,
a highly venomous pit viper. They detect movement using special sensors
on the sides of their head, called pits. That's where their name comes from.

Anna's Eighty-Eight has a pattern on its wings
that resembles this number.
Can you find it?

This is an **Amazon lava lizard**, he won't hurt you.
He will do push-ups to make himself look bigger
or drop his tail if caught, for a quick escape.
Like most lizards, his tail grows back in just a few weeks.

Do you smell something musky?
There must be a jaguar close by.

These are **coatís,** ring-tailed climbers
who are members of the raccoon family.
Like raccoons, they are omnivores and eat frogs,
birds' eggs, insects and berries.

Coatís live in big groups called bands.
When pregnant, the mother leaves the band to make a nest
in the treetops. A few weeks later, once her kittens begin to climb,
like these ones, they'll rejoin the band.

Remember how monkeys' prehensile tails can hold onto branches?
The **tapir** is a unique hooved animal with a prehensile snout!
They use their snout to reach and grasp in all directions.
This helps them locate the best plants and berries.

Tapir babies are born with spots and stripes that help them
hide in the tall grass. That's another great example of?

Natural camouflage, that's right. Gosh, you're good.
Wait! Junior Ranger, speaking of camouflage,
you're never going to believe this! Come, this way…

Junior Ranger, we did it! Together, we found not just one,
but several **jaguars**, which is very special.
Called yaguareté in Spanish and in Guaraní,
these are the biggest cats in the Americas, third largest in the world.
They look like their speedy African relative, the leopard;
but jaguars are bigger, stronger, and not nearly as fast.

Raised by their mother, cubs leave the den to hunt and eat meat when they are just three months old. These ones must be older or else they wouldn't be hanging out with that large male. Their mom is taking a nap, she's resting before she goes hunting tonight.

Jaguars have unique patterns of spots, called markings. Their markings are what make them so hard to find in the rainforest. Just like us, no two jaguars are exactly alike.

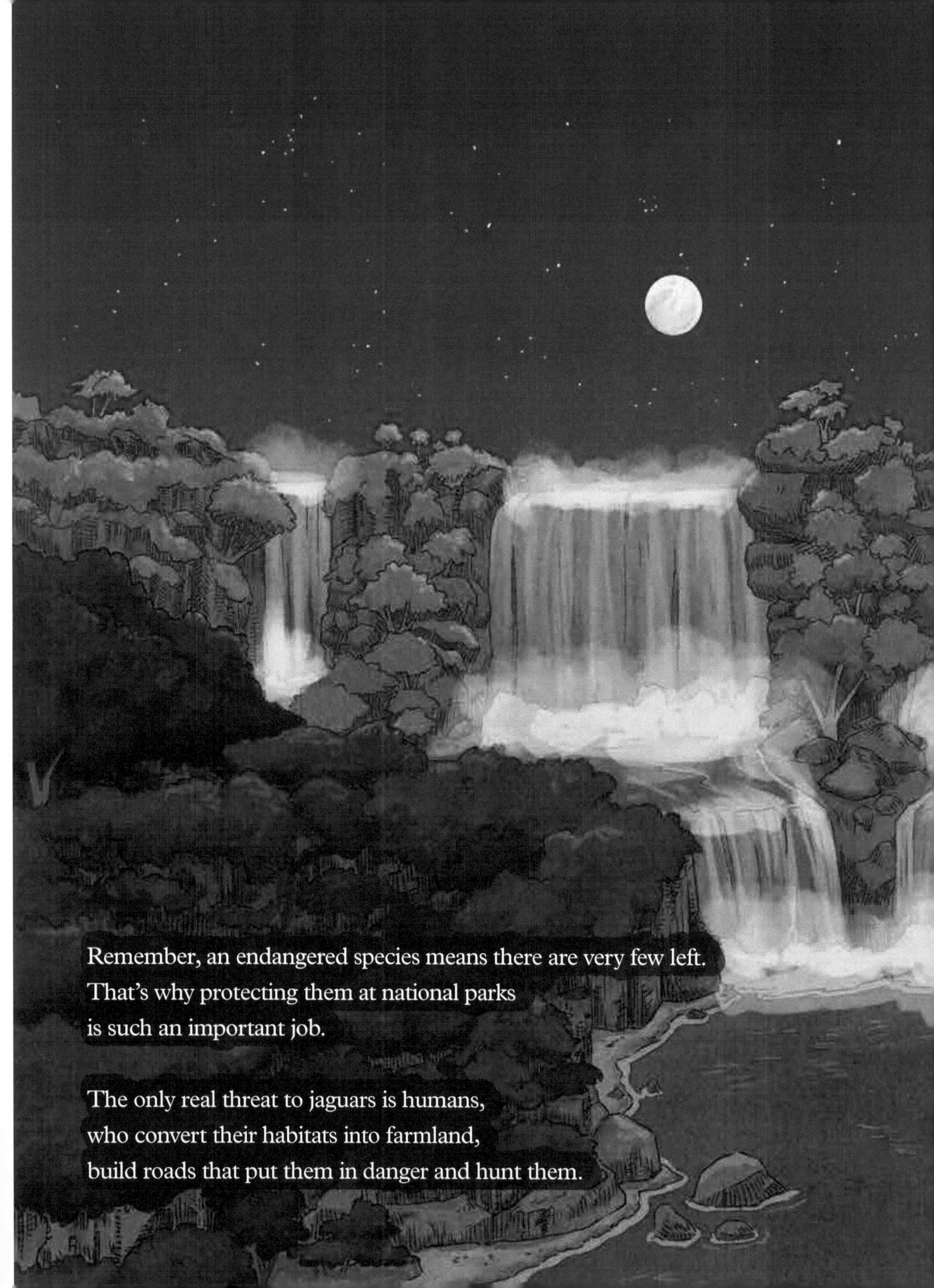

Remember, an endangered species means there are very few left.
That's why protecting them at national parks
is such an important job.

The only real threat to jaguars is humans,
who convert their habitats into farmland,
build roads that put them in danger and hunt them.

Can you believe we saw not just one, but several jaguars?
They can be so hard to spot, especially since there are so few.
Plus, they are really good at hiding, aren't they?

Curious kids who like to learn are the best kind of visitors!
Thanks for joining me and for being such a big help today.
Now you can practice being a park ranger and share
the fauna facts you learned with your friends and family.

I still have many parks to patrol, so I hope you'll join me
on my next adventure here in Argentina.
Be sure to bring a sweater and a big winter coat, it's going to be very chilly!

You did a great job, Junior Ranger. Hasta pronto, see you soon!

Fun Facts: Fauna of Iguazú.

Giant River Otters make all sorts of special sounds. High-pitched squeaks, coos and whistles are some of the noises they use to communicate with their group, called a bevy.

Caiman use the air temperature to regulate their bodies, unlike most animals. That means that if the air is cold, their hearts will beat faster to keep them warm. When it is hot, they can slow their heart-rate, which helps them stay cool.

Capybaras are excellent swimmers. They can stay underwater for up to five minutes and even sleep in the water. When submerged, their ears fold and seal so they don't get water in them, doesn't that sound that nice?

Jaguar's markings feature a ring of black spots, called a rosette, with more spots inside. The rosette is unique to each animal, like a fingerprint.

Ant-eaters tongues are 18 in. long when fully extended and can go in and out of their mouth over 100 times a minute. That makes them the speediest eaters in the rainforest!

An adult **capuchin** can jump as far as 9 feet from one branch to another. That's how long most hammocks are and that's a really big jump!

Junior Ranger Rainforest Review

What do you remember?
This is not a test, **it is a fun way** to go over what we learned today!
You are always welcome to go back and visit the animals if you would like.

---

1. What baby animal lines up their strip to match their moms and become nearly invisible to predators?

- Baby parrots
- Baby ant-eaters
- Baby caimans

2. Jaguars like water, but do most felines like getting wet?

- Yes, of course.
- No way!

3. We saw a butterfly with a design on its wing that looks like a number. Can you remember what it was called?

- Anna's Eighty Eight
- Julia's Twenty Four
- Murphy's One Two Three

4. Is it possible for two jaguars to be identical?

- Sure, why not?
- Nope, every jaguar's spots are different.

5. What part of a tapir's body is prehensile or can grasp like a hand?

- Its leg
- Its tail
- Its snout

Extra Credit:

- What color are MALE howler monkeys?
- What is the smallest raptor called?
- What animal carries her young in her mouth?

Olivia Stanfield

Olivia loves books and has always found her best friends among the covers of a book and the animal kingdom. She resides in Buenos Aires, Argentina where she has lived for many years.

An budding biologist in her student days and a life-long conservationist who hails from from Fauquier County, Virginia, Olivia wishes to bring to the unique fauna of her adopted homeland to young readers in the Northern Hemisphere. She hopes learning about wildlife in an engaging matter motivates future fans of national parks, both in Argentina and in the United States, to practice stewardship of these beautiful spaces and their inhabitants.

A lifelong student of literature, Olivia holds BAs in French and English Literature from the University of Virginia as well as a Master's in Social Policy in Developing Countries from the London School of Economics. When she is not writing, she can be found enjoying the company of her family and that of her many un-exotic pets or planning their next Argentine road-trip.

Kit Turner

With a lifelong fascination for wildlife, Kit brings animals to life through a style that blends naturalism with expressive details. His illustrations are crafted to inspire wonder in young readers, introducing them to unique creatures and the importance of the natural world. Kit hopes each piece sparks curiosity and respect for animals, encouraging children to learn more about our planet's incredible inhabitants.

Kit has studied animals through art for over ten years and holds a BA in Illustration. When he's not drawing he's creating elaborate enclosures for the many reptiles and amphibians that live in his studio.
Dream jobs for Kit would be projects that actively contribute to wildlife conservation and allow him to draw lesser known animals and plant life.

You can find Kit: on Tiktok (@kit.turner), Instagram (@kitturnerillu) and on his website **www.kitturnerillustration.com**

Answers
1. Baby ant-eaters 2. No way! 3. Anna's Eighty Eight,
4. No, every jaguar's spots are different, 5. Its snout
Extra Credit *black, *pearl kite *broad-nosed caiman

www.ingramcontent.com/pod-product-compliance
Lightning Source LLC
Chambersburg PA
CBHW061147030426

42335CB00002B/134